Architecture:

An Image for America

Edited and Introduced
by
Pat Perrin

The Green Dragon Tavern in Boston was built around 1770, prior to the movement to create "an image for America."

Discovery Enterprises, Ltd.
Carlisle, Massachusetts

© Discovery Enterprises, Ltd., Carlisle, MA 1998

ISBN 1-57960-010-7 paperback edition
Library of Congress Catalog Card Number 97-77595

10   9   8   7   6   5   4   3   2   1

Printed in the United States of America

Subject Reference Guide:

Architecture: An Image for America
Edited and Introduced by Pat Perrin

Architecture — U. S. History

U. S. Capitol — U. S. History

Thomas Jefferson — Architecture

Photos/Illustrations:

Cover illustration: The White House, c.1886,
and from the same source: title page, page 15 (bottom),
and page 32 from Edmund V. Gillon, Jr., ed., *Pictorial Archive
of Early Illustrations and Views of American Architecture*,
Dover Publications: NY, 1971.

Library of Congress: pp. 7, 33, 34, 37

National Archives: pp. 12, 17, 55, 56, 60, 62

Other illustrations are credited where they appear in the text.

Table of Contents

What is architecture anyway?

*Is it the vast collection of the various buildings
which have been built to please the varying
tastes of the various lords of mankind?*

*I think not. No, I know that architecture is life;
or at least it is life itself taking form and therefore
it is the truest record of life as it was lived
in the world yesterday, as it is lived today
or ever will be lived.*

— Frank Lloyd Wright

An American Architecture
Edgar Kaufmann, ed.
New York: Horizon Press, 1955

Introduction:
Before the American Image

by
Pat Perrin

Take a look around Washington, D.C. in person or in pictures. What do you think of all those columns, domes, and other bits and pieces translated from Greek and Roman temples? (For that matter, you'll see pretty much the same styles in the capital cities of most states.) For a long time, those were thought to supply the appropriate image for government buildings, banks, and even homes in the United States. But other ideas about building prevailed before anyone tried to decide how America should look.

The first preoccupation of European settlers in North America was, of course, survival. The earliest of the newcomers came ill-prepared even to build shelter. Without adequate tools or trained carpenters and masons, they did not live very comfortably. They burrowed into hillsides and put up rough roofs that usually did not keep out the rain. Their dugouts, sod huts, and ramshackle constructions were far less adequate than the Native American skin tipis and bark huts.

Source: John Smith, *Advertisements for the Unexperienced Planters of New England, or Anywhere*, London, 1631. Cited in James Marston Fitch, *American Building: The Forces That Shape It*, Boston: Houghton Mifflin, 1948, pp. 2-3.

When I first went to Virginia, I well remember we did hang an awning to three or four trees to shadow us from the sun; our walls were rails of wood, our seats unhewed trees til we cut planks, our Pulpit a bar of wood nailed to two neighboring trees. In foul weather we shifted into an old rotten tent; for we had no better....This was our Church, til we built a homely thing like a barn....The best of our houses [were] of the like curiosity but for the most part far worse workmanship, that could neither well defend [from] wind nor rain.

5

The settlers soon began to request that skilled craftsmen join their community, and bring decent tools with them. Within a few years the newcomers were building wood-frame, log, brick, and stone structures according to techniques they had used in Europe. A long-lasting conviction developed that theirs was the only real building on an otherwise empty continent.

Source: James H. Simpson, *Navaho Expedition: Journal of a Military Reconnaissance from Santa Fe, New Mexico to the Navaho Country Made in 1849 by Lieutenant James H. Simpson,* edited and annotated by Frank McNitt, Norman, Oklahoma, University of Oklahoma Press, 1964, p 56.

———————————————

The great historian Robertson, it is said, has stated (I have not his works near me to verify the fact) that "there is not in all the extent of New Spain any monument or vestige of a building more ancient than the conquest; that the temple of *Cholula* is nothing but a mound of solid earth, without any facing, or any steps, covered with grass and shrubs; and that the houses of the people of Mexico are mere huts, built with turf or branches of trees, like those of the rudest Indians." However applicable this may be to the ancient remains said to have been found in New Spain—and I have no reason, from my reading, to believe it so—it certainly cannot be predicated of those discovered on the Rio Chaco.

Others acknowledged—as Lieutenant Simpson suspected—that the Aztec cities conquered by the Spanish were as impressive as anything to be found in Europe. Later, monumental ruins left by earlier Maya, Olmec, and Toltec civilizations were also discovered in what is now Mexico and Central America.

Even so, there seemed at first to be a lack of any permanent Native American building in North America. Various explorers did speak of the ruins of stone buildings at Chaco Canyon, in the territory of New Mexico. Simpson's brigade was part of the armed forces protecting the territories ceded to the United States after the Mexican War (1846-1848).

The buildings of the ancient Anasazi culture at Chaco Canyon and Mesa Verde date from around 1000 A.D. Although both areas are now national parks, we still know very little about the builders.

Sophisticated structures of Mesa Verde, in Colorado, were probably abandoned in the 1400s.

Simpson's journals describe his first views of two of the numerous ruins at Chaco Canyon.

Source: James H. Simpson, *op cit.*, pp. 36, 47.

After partaking of some refreshments I started off, with high expectations—my assistants, the Messrs. Kern, accompanying me—to examine the ruins of Pueblo Pintado. We found them to more than answer our expectations. Forming one structure, and built of tabular pieces of hard, fine-grained compact gray sandstone (a material entirely unknown in the present architecture of New Mexico), to which the atmosphere has imparted a reddish tinge, the layers or beds being not thicker than three inches, and sometimes as thin as one-fourth of an inch, it discovers in the masonry a combination of science and art which can only be referred to a higher stage of civilization and refinement than is discoverable in the works of Mexicans or Pueblos of the present day. Indeed, so beautifully diminutive and true are the details of the structure as to cause it, at a little distance, to have all the appearance of a magnificent piece of mosaic work.

Two or three hundred yards down the cañon we met another old pueblo in ruins, called *Pueblo Bonito*. This pueblo, though not so beautiful in the arrangement of the details of its masonry as Pueblo Pintado, is yet superior to it in point of preservation. The circuit of its walls is about thirteen hundred feet. Its present elevation shows that it has had at least four stories of apartments. The number of rooms on the ground floor at present discernible is one hundred and thirty-nine. In this enumeration, however, are not included the apartments which are not distinguishable in the east portion of the pueblo, and which would probably swell the number to about two hundred. There, then, having been at least four stories of rooms, and supposing the horizontal depth of the edifice to have been uniform from top to bottom, or in other words, not of a retreating terrace form on the court side, it is not unreasonable to infer that the original number of rooms was as many as eight hundred. But…there must be a reduction from this number of one range of rooms for every story after the first; and this would lessen the number to six hundred and forty-one.

Even before the new Americans saw the huge stone buildings in the west, some had noticed a different kind of monumental structure in eastern and central areas—often right under their feet. Tens of thousands of earthen mounds had been built by a number of different Native American cultures, some as long as 5000 years ago. These structures ranged from burial mounds to complex earthworks that seem to have been ceremonial in nature.

European settlers usually considered the mounds defensive structures and sometimes casually labeled them the remains of Spanish forts. Those who did recognize the gigantic structures as a kind of architecture tried to assign their origins to various foreign cultures.

The earthworks caught the attention of George Washington and Thomas Jefferson, as well as others who had interests in archeology and in Native American traditions. Antiquarian societies were formed to map the monuments. Nevertheless, many of the earthworks disappeared beneath roads, canals, farms, and cities.

Great Serpent Mound, near Portsmouth, Ohio, was built around 1000 A.D.

European settlers in North America built in the style of their homelands—Spanish-style missions and homes in Florida and on the west coast, and English state houses in the colonies. The influence of English architect Christopher Wren and his students was particularly strong in Williamsburg. But soon after the Revolution, American builders began thinking about an image of our own.

In the memoirs and correspondence that follows, you'll see some variations in spelling. I have kept the words just as they appear in each document.

Thomas Jefferson and the Virginia Capitol

Thomas Jefferson was one of the first to be concerned about a suitable image for the new country. He was as interested in what buildings had to say about a culture as he was about their use. As a scholar, he knew about the architectural styles of past cultures. As an American, he wanted the buildings of this new country to express democratic ideals. And, as a politician, he was sometimes able to get things done the way he wanted.

On England

Long after 1776, Jefferson continued to think of England as America's enemy. He lived in Paris from 1784-1789, first as a commissioner then as minister to France. After making a trip to England in 1786, Jefferson wrote to his friend John Page that May.

Source: Thomas Jefferson, *Writings*, edited by Merrill D. Peterson, New York: Library Classics of the United States, 1984, p. 854.

The city of London, tho' handsomer than Paris, is not so handsome as Philadelphia. Their architecture is in the most wretched stile I ever saw, not meaning to except America where it is bad, nor even Virginia where it is worse than in any other part of America, which I have seen....

Architecture in Virginia

It was not surprising that Jefferson also disapproved of the architecture he saw in America, since it was English in style. His Notes on the State of Virginia *was written in 1782 in response to queries made by the secretary of the French legation in Philadelphia. Jefferson later revised the material and had it printed in Paris in 1784.*

Source: Thomas Jefferson, *Writings, op cit.,* pp. 278-9.

The private buildings are very rarely constructed of stone or brick, much the greatest portion being of scantling and boards, plastered with lime. It is impossible to devise things more ugly, uncomfortable, and happily more perishable. There are two or three plans, on one of which, according to its size, most of the houses in the State are built. The poorest people built huts of logs, laid horizontally in pens, stopping the interstices with mud. These are warmer in winter, and cooler in summer, than the most expensive construction of scantling and plank....

The only public buildings worthy of mention are the capitol, the palace, the college, and the hospital for lunatics, all of them in Williamsburg, heretofore the seat of our government. The capitol is a light and airy structure, with a portico in front of two orders, the lower of which, being Doric,[1] is tolerably just in its proportions and ornaments....The upper is Ionic, much too small for that on which it is mounted, its ornaments not proper to the order, nor proportioned within themselves. It is crowned with a pediment, which is too high for its span. Yet, on the whole, it is the most pleasing piece of architecture we have. The palace is not handsome without, but it is spacious and commodious within, is prettily situated, and with the grounds annexed to it, is capable of being made an elegant seat. The college and hospital are rude, mis-shapen piles, which, but that they have roofs, would be taken for brick-kilns. There are no other public buildings but churches and court-houses, in which no attempts are made at elegance. Indeed, it would not be easy to execute such an attempt, as a workman could scarcely be found capable of drawing an order. The genius of architecture seems to have shed its maledictions over this land.

---

[1] Doric and Ionic orders are types of columns used on Greek and Roman buildings (as is the Corinthian order, which will be mentioned later).

Buildings are often erected, by individuals, of considerable expense. To give these symmetry and taste, would not increase their cost. It would only change the arrangement of the materials, the form and combination of the members. This would often cost less than the burthen of barbarous ornaments with which these buildings are sometimes charged. But the first principles of the art are unknown, and there exists scarcely a model among us sufficiently chaste to give an idea of them. Architecture being one of the fine arts, and as such within the department of a professor of the college, according to the new arrangement, perhaps a spark may fall on some young subjects of natural taste, kindle up their genius, and produce a reformation in this elegant and useful art. But all we shall do in this way will produce no permanent improvement to our country, while the unhappy prejudice prevails that houses of brick or stone are less wholesome than those of wood.

A Roman Image for Virginia

When Jefferson helped design the government for his new nation, he often referred to the ideals of the Roman Republic. So it wasn't surprising that he thought the status of the arts in Virginia would be improved by an example of architecture in the ancient Roman style. Before he went abroad in 1784, Jefferson had already presented the House of Delegates with his idea for a new national Capitol modeled on a Roman temple. While Jefferson was in Paris, he saw and admired the artwork of Jacques-Louis David, who used Roman images to symbolize the revolutionary spirit in France.

In 1779, when the Virginia General Assembly passed an act providing land for a new state capitol building in Richmond, they sought Jefferson's advice. In 1821 he related the story in his autobiography.

Source: Thomas Jefferson, *Writings, op cit.*, p 41.

I was written to in 1785 (being then in Paris) by directors appointed to superintend the building of a Capitol in Richmond, to advise them as to a plan, and to add to it one of a Prison. Thinking it a favorable opportunity of introducing into the State an example of architecture, in the classic style of antiquity, and the Maison Quarrée of Nismes, an ancient Roman temple, being considered as the most perfect model existing of what may be called Cubic architecture, I applied to M. Clerissault, who had published drawings of the Antiquities of Nismes, to have me a model of the building made in stucco, only changing the order from Corinthian to Ionic, on account of the difficulty of the Corinthian capitals....This was executed by the artist whom Choiseul Gouffier had carried with him to Constantinople, and employed, while Ambassador there in making those beautiful models of the remains of Grecian architecture which are to be seen at Paris. To adapt the exterior to our use, I drew a plan for the interior, with the apartments necessary for legislative, executive, and judiciary purposes; and accommodated in their size and distribution to the form and dimensions of the building. These were forwarded to the Directors, in 1786, and were carried into execution, with some variations, not for the better, the most important of which, however, admit of future correction.

While Jefferson was in Paris, he wrote several letters to James Madison and other friends about the Maison Quarrée. On September 20, 1785, he described his choice of design to Madison:

Source: Thomas Jefferson, *Writings, op cit.,* p 829.

We took for our model what is called the Maison quarrée of Nismes, one of the most beautiful, if not the most beautiful and precious morsel of architecture left us by antiquity. It was built by Caius and Lucius Caesar and repaired by Louis XIV, and has the suffrage of all the judges of architecture who have seen it, as yielding to no one of the beautiful monuments of Greece, Rome, Palmyra and Balbec which late travellers have communicated to us. It is very simple, but it is noble beyond expression, and would have done honor to our country as presenting to travellers a morsel of taste in our infancy promising much for our maturer age.

On January 26, 1786, Jefferson described his work on the project in a letter to James Buchanan and William Hay.

Source: Thomas Jefferson, *Writings, op cit.*, pp. 845-6.

I had the honor of writing to you on the receipt of your orders to procure draughts for the public buildings, and again on the 13th of August. In the execution of these orders two methods of proceeding presented themselves to my mind. The one was to leave to some architect to draw an external according to his fancy, in which way experience shows that about once in a thousand times a pleasing form is hit upon; the other was to take some model already devised and approved by the general suffrage of the world. I had no hesitation in deciding that the latter was best, nor after the decision was there any doubt what model to take. There is at Nismes in the South of France a building, called the *Maison Quarrée*, erected in the time of the Caesars, and which is allowed without contradiction to be the most perfect and precious remain of antiquity in existence. Its superiority over anything at Rome, in Greece, at Balbec or Palmyra is allowed on all hands; and this single object has placed Nismes in the general tour of travellers. Having not yet had leisure to visit it, I could only judge of it from drawings, and from the relation of numbers who had been to see it. I determined therefore to adopt this model, & to have all its proportions justly drewed....We know that the *Maison Quarrée* has pleased universally for near 2000 years.

Engraving made by archeologist Charles-Louis Clérisseau of Maison Quarrée, from Antiquities de la France, *Paris, 1778.*

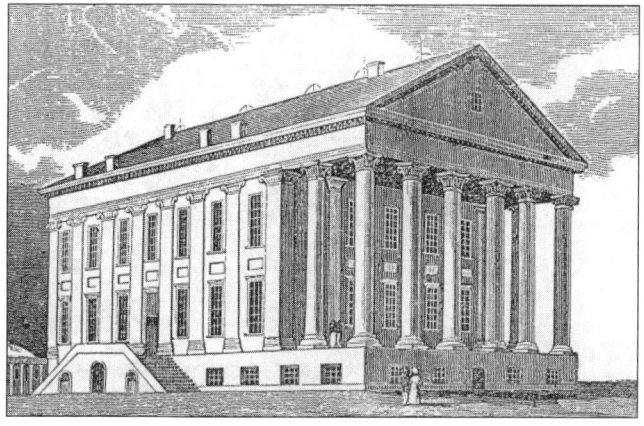

The Virginia Capitol, designed by Thomas Jefferson. (Built in 1789, illustration c. 1848)

Jefferson finally did get to see the Maison Quarrée in 1787, and clearly was not disappointed. He was, however, not pleased with the general treatment of such ruins in France, as he explained in a letter to his friend Madame de Tessé.

Source: Thomas Jefferson, *Writings, op cit.,* pp. 891-3.

Here I am, Madam, gazing whole hours at the Maison quarrée, like a lover at his mistress....

From Lyons to Nismes I have been nourished with the remains of Roman grandeur. They have always brought you to my mind, because I know your affection for whatever is Roman and noble. At Vienne I thought of you. But I am glad you were not there; for you would have seen me more angry than, I hope, you will ever see me. The Praetorian palace, as it is called, comparable, for its fine proportions, to the Maison quarrée, defaced by the barbarians who have converted it to its present purpose, its beautiful fluted Corinthian columns cut out in part, to make space for Gothic windows, and hewed down, in the residue, to the plane of the building, was enough, you must admit, to disturb my composure. At Orange too, I thought of you. I was sure you had seen with pleasure, the sublime triumphal arch of Marius at the entrance of the city. I went then to the Arenae. Would you believe, Madam, that in this eighteenth century, in France, under the reign of Louis XVI. they are at this moment pulling down the circular wall of this superb remain, to pave a road? And that too from a hill which is itself an entire mass of stone, just as fit and more accessible?...

These, Madam, are my opinions; but I wish to know yours, which, I am sure, will be better....I am immersed in antiquities from morning to night. For me, the city of Rome is actually existing in all the splendor of its empire....If I am sometimes induced to look forward to the eighteenth century, it is only when recalled to it by the recollection of your goodness and friendship, and by those sentiments of sincere esteem and respect, with which I have the honor to be, Madam, your most obedient and most humble servant....

The Virginia Capitol was built more or less according to Thomas Jefferson's designs. When he returned to America, Jefferson was made Secretary of State under President George Washington. After altercations with Secretary of the Treasury, Alexander Hamilton, Jefferson resigned that position in December of 1793. During his brief retirement, he redesigned and began to rebuild his home, Monticello. He also designed courthouses and other buildings in Virginia. His most elegant architectural designs may be those for the University of Virginia, which opened in 1825, the year before Jefferson died. All were based on Roman (and interpretations of Roman) buildings.

Colonnades at the dormitories of the University of Virginia.

While he was Secretary of State and President, Jefferson was deeply involved with the development of an appropriate image for the new Capitol of the United States.

A Classical Capitol for the New Capital

During the Italian Renaissance,[2] the term "classical" was used to identify the art and architecture of Greece or Rome. The classical style was associated with the idea of an underlying order in the world that could be discovered by the powers of reason. The intervening Medieval period was viewed as a time of chaos. The notion of control over one's world had a great deal of appeal in eighteenth-century America.

How to Pick a Winner

In July of 1790, the U.S. House of Representatives chose a site near Georgetown for a new federal city. George Washington and Thomas Jefferson (then Secretary of State) chose the French urban designer Pierre L'Enfant to develop a plan for the city. They also appointed a board of Commissioners to oversee the development of the city. Although the relationship between the Commissioners and L'Enfant was a stormy one, the design of a new city did begin to emerge.

On Jefferson's recommendation, the Commissioners held a competition for the design of the Capitol building. In March 1792, they placed an ad in leading newspapers. Few of those who entered the exhibition were professional architects. Many of the submissions were in the English Georgian style so hated by Jefferson. The best design came from Stephen Hallet, who had been an architect in his native France. Still, the committee wasn't completely satisfied with Hallet's design, so they asked for revisions. For six months, Hallet reworked his ideas according to the recommendations of the committee. Then Dr. William Thornton sent in a sketch and asked to be permitted to submit plans. The plans didn't show up, but eventually Dr. Thornton did. He arrived with a letter in hand from President Washington to the Commissioners.

---

[2] The fourteenth through the sixteenth centuries.

A PREMIUM

Of a LOT, in the City, to be designated by impartial Judges, and FIVE HUNDRED DOLLARS, or a MEDAL of that Value, at the Option of the Party, will be given by the Commissioners of the Federal Buildings, to the Person who, before the Fifteenth Day of July, 1792, shall produce to them the most approved PLAN, if adopted by them, for a CAPI-TOL, to be erected in this City; and TWO HUNDRED and FIFTY DOLLARS, or a MEDAL, for the Plan deemed next in merit to the one they shall adopt. The Building to be of Brick, and to contain the following Apartments, to wit:

A Conference Room, a Room for the Representatives, sufficient to accommodate 300 Persons each,
A Lobby or Antichamber to the latter.
A Senate-Room of 1200 square Feet Area,
An Antichamber or Lobby to the latter.
These Rooms to be of full Elevation.
Twelve Rooms of 600 square Feet Area each,
for Committee-Rooms, and Clerks' Offices,
to be of Half the Elevation of the former.

Drawings will be expected of the Ground-Plans, Elevations of each Front, and Sections through the Building, in such Directions as may be necessary to explain the internal Structure; and an Estimate of the cubic Feet of Brick-Work composing the whole Mass of Walls.

Copy of the ad placed by the Commissioners in March 1792

Source: George Washington, January 31, 1793, in *The Papers of Thomas Jefferson*, edited by John Catanzariti, Vol. 25, 1 January to 10 May 1793, Princeton, New Jersey: Princeton University Press, 1992, pp. 107-8. The words in brackets were added between the lines by Washington.

I have had under consideration Mr. Hallet's plans for the capitol, which undoubtedly have a great deal of merit. Doctor Thornton has also given me a view of his. These last come

19

forward under some very advantageous circumstances. The grandeur, simplicity, and beauty of the exterior, the propriety with which the apartments are distributed, and economy in the mass of the whole structure, will, I doubt not give it a preference in your eyes, as it has done in mine, and those of several others whom I have consulted [and are deemed men of Skill and taste in Architecture]. I have therefore thought it better to give the Doctor time to finish his plan, and for this purpose to delay till your next meeting a final decision. Some difficulty arises with respect to Mr. Hallet, who you know was in some degree led into his plan by ideas we all expressed to him. This ought not to induce us to prefer it to a better: but while he is liberally rewarded for the time and labor he has expended on it, his feelings should be saved and soothed as much as possible. I leave it to yourselves how best to prepare him for the possibility that the Doctor's plan may be preferred to his. Some ground for this will be furnished you by the occasion you [probably] will have for recourse to him as to the interior of the apartments, and the taking him into service at a fixed allowance, and I understand that his necessities render it material that he should know what his allowance is to be.

The following day, February 1, 1793, Thomas Jefferson sent a letter to Daniel Carroll, one of the commissioners, expressing similar sentiments.

Source: Thomas Jefferson, *The Papers of Thomas Jefferson, op. cit.,* p. 110.

Doctr. Thornton's plan of a Capitol has been produced, and has so captivated the eyes and judgment of all as to leave no doubt you will prefer it when it shall be exhibited to you; as no doubt exists here of it's preference over all which have been produced, and among it's admirers no one is more decided than him whose decision is most important. It is simple, noble, beautiful, excellently distributed, and moderate in size. The purpose of this letter is to apprise you of this sentiment. A just respect for the right of approbrobation in the Commissioners will prevent any formal decision in the President till the plan shall be laid before you and be approved by you. The Doctor will go with it to your meeting in the beginning of March. In the mean time, the interval of *apparent* doubt, may be improved for soothing the mind of poor Hallet, whose merit and distresses interest every one for his tranquility and pecuniary relief. I have taken the liberty of making these private intimations, thinking you would wish to know the true state of the sentiments here on this subject, and am with sincere respect & esteem for your collegues & yourself Dear Sir your most obedt. humble servt

TH: JEFFERSON

Thornton's was the only design for the Capitol that displayed the noble Roman style so admired by Jefferson and Washington. And with those two letters of recommendation, it was obvious that Thornton's design would be chosen. The Commissioners replied to Jefferson on February 7th.

Source: *The Papers of Thomas Jefferson, op. cit.,* p. 152.

Tho' we are much pleased, that we shall at length be furnished with the plan of a Capitol so highly satisfactory to the President, and all who have seen it, we feell sensibly for poor Hallet, and shall do every thing in our power to sooth him. We hope he may be usefully employed notwithstanding.

Construction and Contention

At first, the Commissioners wrote a letter to Hallett saying that neither he nor Thornton had actually won the first prize—and that while Thornton would receive the $500 and lot, Hallett would also receive $500 plus the cash value of a lot. In April, they formally awarded the prize to Thornton. Perhaps embarrassed over stringing Hallet along, the Commissioners made him Supervisor of Construction. Hallet soon began to point out flaws in Thornton's designs. (Apparently the floor plan didn't actually match up with the drawing of the exterior.) It was just the beginning of a long struggle to produce a building for the United States Capitol. In his fictional Memoirs of Aaron Burr, *Author Gore Vidal describes the scant progress that had been made by 1801.*

Source: Gore Vidal, *Burr*, New York: Random House, 1973, p. 229.

At the beginning of March, Theodosia, her husband and I arrived at the new capital city (which lacked both city and capitol). On a slight rise in the wilderness was the Senate chamber. Some yards distant was a small ellipse-shaped building, recently thrown together to shelter the House of Representatives and known to its unhappy occupants as "The Oven." Between the two buildings was a covered passageway. That was all there was to the Capitol. Today's noble brown dome was only a dream.

Close to the unfinished Capitol a few dozen houses formed the core to the city....

A mile and a half from the Capitol, the Treasury building was nearly complete, as was its neighbour, the executive mansion. Connecting Capitol and president's house was a long cow-trail on either side of which Jefferson was to plant several rows of rather forlorn-looking trees, eagerly explaining to anyone who would listen how exactly like a Paris boulevard it looked.

Latrobe Takes On the Capitol—and Thornton

Thornton remained a Commissioner until 1803 and during that time several architects came and went. Jefferson, now president, despaired of completing a suitable structure. He opened a search for someone who could do the job. He hired Henry Latrobe, who had been trained in England and who had already attracted attention for his classical-style public buildings in Virginia. Robert Mills, an architect who was later to do some work on the Capitol himself (and design the Washington Monument) was a student of Latrobe's. In an unfinished essay titled "The Progress of Architecture in Virginia" Mills introduces Latrobe.

Source: Don Gifford, editor, *The Literature of Architecture: The Evolution of Architectural Theory and Practice in Nineteenth-Century America*, New York: E.P. Dutton, 1966, pp. 86-87.

In 1791 Benjamin Henry Latrobe, Esq. [27 years old], an eminent English architect and engineer, came from England to reside in Virginia. This gentleman was the son of the sculptor of the great Zenzendorf (the founder of the Moravian sect of Christians). Mr. Latrobe was led to Virginia by the expectation of inheriting a large patrimonial estate there belonging to his father, but was disappointed in its value. About this period the penitentiary system was introduced into Virginia, and Mr. Latrobe was employed to design and superintend its erection. This building was designed upon architectural principles; it was the best constructed and arranged prison then extant in the Union. In 1791, Mr. Latrobe was called to Philadelphia to design and erect the Bank of Pennsylvania—a beautiful marble structure of the temple form after that of Theseus in Athens....

Latrobe explained some of the shortcomings he saw in Thornton's designs to Thomas Jefferson. Then he apparently attempted to explain those problems to Thornton, himself. On February 27th, 1804, Latrobe wrote to Jefferson about that meeting.

Source: Benjamin Latrobe, *The Correspondence and Miscellaneous Papers of Benjamin Henry Latrobe*, Vol. 1, 1784-1804, edited by Edward C. Carter II, New Haven: Yale University Press, 1984, p. 437.

I judged very ill in going to Thornton. In a few peremptory words, he, in fact, told me, that no difficulties existed in his plan, but such as were made by those who were too ignorant to remove them and though these were not exactly his words, his expressions, his tone, his manner, and his absolute refusal to devote a few minutes to discuss the subject spoke his meaning even more strongly and offensively than I have expressed it. I left him with an assurance that I should not be the person to attempt to remove them, and had I had immediate possession of pen, ink, and paper, I should have directly solicited your permission to resign my office.

I owe however too much to you to risk by so hasty a step, the miscarriage of any measure you may wish to promote, and I shall devote as before my utmost endeavors to excite the disposition in the Committee, to which I am summoned tomorrow morning, in favor of the appropriation.

In respect to the plan itself, it is impossible to convey by words or drawings to the mind of any man, that impression of the difficulties in execution which 20 Years experience creates in the mind of a professional man. I fear I have said already too much for the respect I owe to your opinions, though much too little for my own conviction....My wish to avoid vexation, trouble, and enmities is weak, compared to my desire to be placed among those whom you regard with approbation and friendship. If you therefore, *under all circumstances*, conceive that my services can still be useful, I place myself entirely at your disposal. I am with sincere respect Your faithful hble. Servt.

B. Henry Latrobe

Jefferson must have been eager to get the construction project moving again. In his reply of February 28, he pointed out that the competition for a design for the President's house (the White House) had already produced a completed building.

Source: Benjamin Latrobe, *op cit.*, p. 439.

I am sorry the explanations attempted between Dr. Thornton and yourself on the manner of finishing the chamber of the house of representatives have not succeeded. At the original establishment of this place advertisements were published many months offering premiums for the best plans for a Capitol and President's house. Many were sent in. A council was held by Genl. Washington with the board of Commissioners and after very mature examination two were preferred and the premiums given to their authors Doctr. Thornton and Hobans, and the plans were decided on. Hobans', has been executed. On Dr. Thornton's plan of the Capitol the North wing has been executed, and the South raised one story. In order to get along with any public undertaking it is necessary that some stability of plan be observed. Nothing impedes progress so much as perpetual changes of design....

Latrobe's February 28th, 1804, response to Jefferson made some of the architect's anxieties clear.

Source: Benjamin Latrobe, *op. cit.*, pp. 441-443.

The circumstances that attend the conflict between my wish to promote your views respecting the Capitol, and my conviction of the necessity for forming a plan different from that which is now said by Dr. Thornton to be the plan approved by General Washington are among the most unpleasant which I have ever had to struggle with. It cannot in my opinion be stated that any plan, that is any *practicable* plan exists, or ever existed....

In a contest, similar to that in which I am engaged, first with Mr. Hallet, then with Mr. Hatfield, Doctor Thornton was victorious. Both these men, men of knowledge, talents, integrity and amiable manners were ruined....[Hatfield] is now starving in Washington, and Hallet was ruined some Years ago....

The Committee have just risen. Their enquiries have been most minute. I produced the plan given me by Doctor Thornton. I mean the ground plan. Its absurdities are still more glaring than its insufficiency as a guide, by which to execute the work. I was asked whether that was the original plan? I said, no, and had I said otherwise I should have failed in my duty to myself and, to truth. I was asked for the original plan? It is not to be found. Whose plan was that which I exhibited? I detailed the authors of the different parts. Is it a good plan? No! What are its faults? I confined myself to the total want of offices and accomodation of every kind. How can they be remedied? By raising the floor one story higher. More questions were asked, and answered agreeably to truth, without fear or self interest, for it is my interest in this city, peaceably to act and speak to every body but yourself, directly contrary to my judgement.

I was desired to put in writing all that I had verbally stated...

In the report which I shall make tomorrow, I shall be under the necessity of speaking the truth as to the history of the plan and the causes of the defects of the building. I am prepared for open war, and shall suffer less by it than I have already done by that conduct that keeps greater talents than I possess out of sight. I shall recommend *nothing*, but *generally say* that all the inconveniences and deficiencies stated, *may be easily remedied* without altering the external appearance of the building....

In his written report to the Commissioners, Latrobe recounted the difficult history of the Capitol to that point.

Source: Benjamin Latrobe, *op. cit.*, pp. 443-445.

To the Chairman of the Committee of the House of Representatives in Congress, to whom was referred the Message of the President of the United States of the 22d of February 1804, transmitting a report of the Surveyor of the Public buildings of the 20th. of February, 1804.

The Report of the Surveyor of the public Buildings

Sir,

In compliance with my duty, and your desire, that I should give you such information respecting the original plan of the Capitol as approved by General Washington, of the accomodations provided therein for the house of Representatives, together with my opinion as to such alterations as might further conduce to render the house as commodious as possible, I beg to submit to you the following report.

By the act of Congress of the 16th. July 1790 establishing the permanent seat of Government, it is enacted, among others, "that the President shall appoint three Commissioners" who shall *"according to such plans as the President shall approve"* &c. "prior to the 1st day of December 1800 provide suitable buildings for the accomodation of Congress" &c.

General Washington, at that time president of the United States did approve the plan of Doctor Thornton, and by that approbation this plan became, as it were, a part of the Law, and ceased to be liable to alteration, untill the act of Congress of 1802-1803, which appropriated 50.000$ towards the completion of the Capitol, and other public purposes, and authorized *"alterations"* in the plan.

Of the plan approved by General Washington no drawing can at present be found among the papers belonging to the office. From the evidence of the foundations which were taken up during the last Season, from some which still remain, and especially from the testimony of all those who were first employed in the execution of the Work, it appears that, it differed from that which is now to be had, in many essential points. The evidence of the books of the Office proves that it was not considered as practicable. As its author was not a professional Man, it was put into the hands of Mr. Hallet, whose knowledge, and talents as a practical architect are proved by his designs, still in the office, that its deficiencies might be corrected. Mr. Hallet however, was not continued in the public service. Mr. Hatfield afterwards succeeded to the superintendance of the Capitol. Of his judicious attempts to correct the radical errors of the original design, as far as it could be understood from the imperfect sketches, which were put into his hands, instances are every where to be found in the North wing of the Capitol; and it is to be regretted that his endeavors, upon the whole, failed, and that the public have lost the benefit of his talents. After the departure of Mr. Hatfield, the public became indebted to Mr. Geo: Blagden, of whose integrity and abilities, as the principal Stone Mason, his work bears honorable testimony, for the excellent execution of the Freestone work of the North wing.

Under the hands of Mr. Hallet, and of Mr. Hatfield, the original design, as far as its erection was attempted, received improvement, and considerable alteration. The various stiles of each architect show themselves in the work, and prove the truth of the preceding statements. The parts belonging to each might be pointed out in detail, if it were interesting or necessary.

When the President of the United States did me the honor to employ me in the direction of the Work, my first endeavor was to procure the drawings necessary to understand and execute the original design; for which purpose I applied to the Author, and received only a ground plan. No information as to the execution of any part of the work, being given by this plan beyond what was already built, I searched the papers in the office, and applied to the persons formerly employed in the Work. I was every where disappointed, *and found that no drawings from which the design could be understood or executed existed*, and that the plan of which I was possessed, independently of several parts being wholly impracticable, did not agree with the foundations which were laid. I was also informed, and the most indisputable evidence was brought before me, to prove, that no sections, or detailed drawings of the building had ever existed excepting those which were from time to time made by Messrs. Hallet and Hatfield, for their own use in the direction of the work.

From what I have said, it is evident, that I am unable to give you any information as to the plan approved by General Washington....

Latrobe's report was published, and on April 23rd, 1804, William Thornton responded quite directly.

Source: Benjamin Latrobe, *op. cit.*, pp. 479-480.

It is with extreme regret that I think myself under the necessity of addressing you, but as I am unwilling to offend any Gentleman without provocation, so am I equally disinclined to receive unnoticed any Insult. Never was my Surprise so much excited as on reading this Day, for the first time, your Letter to the Committee of Congress dated the 28th. of Feby. last. My uniform behaviour to you in the City of Washington I did imagine would have precluded you from offering any thing like insult or even incivility; but I am sorry to be obliged to declare that your Letter to the Committee is, as it respects me, not only ungentlemanly but false. I am Sir with due respect,

W: Thornton

Latrobe wrote back to Thornton on April 28th, outlining specific personal insults and essentially declaring a state of war.

Source: Benjamin Latrobe, *op. cit.*, pp. 481-482.

Open hostility is safer, than insidious friendship. I cannot therefore regret the declaration of War contained in your letter of the 23d. April. For a considerable time I have been convinced that an open rupture with you would be more honorable to me than even that show of good understanding which has prevailed between us....

When I accepted the office which has connected my Character with the successful and honest management of the public Buildings at Washington, I was informed that I had nothing to do with you or your plan. Thinking however that much was due to your feelings, and to your reputation, and perceiving much superior talent, and, as I thought much goodness of heart under the confusion of your conversation, and rubbish of your language, I determined to consult, and advise with you on every thing I did. In this determination I persevered notwithstanding my ill success with you. Those who despise you most in Washington can bear witness to my perseverance in this resolution. My last call upon you is the strongest proof how far I was willing to go. The insulting treatment I received closed all further prospect of amicable arrangement, which I might have expected from your politeness or your understanding.

I now stand on the Ground from which you drove Hallet, and Hatfield to ruin. You may prove victorious against me also; but the contest will not be without spectators. The public shall attend and judge. I shall not court public discussion. It is in my *power* however, more than in my inclination to show you in a more ridiculous light, even, than were I, as is the fashion after such a correspondence, to call you to the field. But you have other accounts of that sort to settle before it can come to my turn. There is a certain advantage which I shall gain by your declared enmity. Your standing in society is such that in proportion to your abuse of me I shall be respected and to your denial of my assertions they will be believed. And you must also be a gainer by the present state of things. Hitherto your detraction has been limited to the circle of those, whom you thought unconnected with me, you can now indulge it without restraint, and wherever you please. I am Sir with due respect &c.

Construction on the Capitol Goes On...and On

Benjamin Latrobe worked on the Capitol from 1803-1817, struggling with Jefferson over changes and with Congress over money, as well as battling with Thornton. Many of the most elegant interior spaces of the Capitol are Latrobe's work. Nevertheless, he was eventually forced to resign due to the disagreements, construction delays, and rising costs.

Instead of sticking to the classical Doric, Ionic, and Corinthian orders for the capitals (heads) of columns, Benjamin Latrobe contributed these uniquely American versions to the Capitol building, featuring corn and tobacco.

In 1818, President James Monroe appointed Boston architect Charles Bulfinch to complete the work. He made his own changes to the existing plans and redesigned the dome according to the desires of Congress for greater monumentality. By 1829 the Capitol had reached a level of completion that held until mid-century. By then, the capital city had developed a distinctly classical appearance.

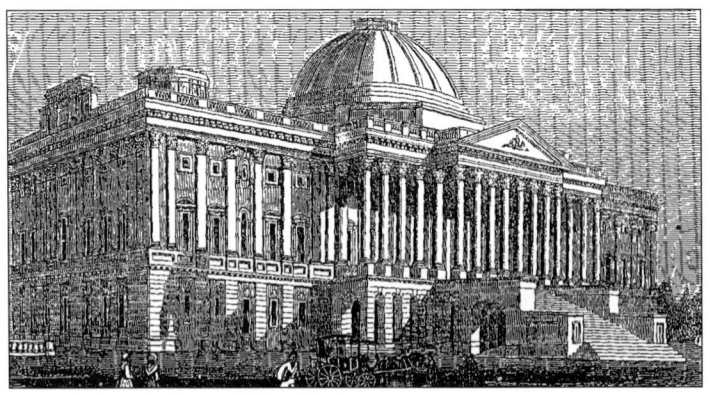

The Capitol as originally completed with Bulfinch's dome.

Henry Adams, a historian (and descendent of two presidents), described Washington about 1850 in his autobiography, first published posthumously in 1918.

Source: Henry Adams, *The Education of Henry Adams*, New York: Penguin Books, 1995, pp. 46-47.

Coming down in the early morning from his bedroom in his grandmother's house—still called the Adams building—in F Street, and venturing out into the air reeking with the thick odor of the catalpa trees, he found himself on an earth-road, or village street, with wheel-tracks meandering from the colonnade of the Treasurey hard by, to the white marble columns and fronts of the Post Office and Patent Office, which faced each other in the distance, like white Greek temples in the abandoned gravel-pits of a deserted Syrian city.

In 1850, Robert Mills and Thomas U. Walter participated in adding extensions to the Capitol building. In 1855, Congress authorized a new dome, the cast-iron structure so familiar to us today. For his model, Walter chose Michelangelo's dome for St. Peters in Rome and Christopher Wren's dome for St. Paul's Cathedral in London. So the dome of the Capitol was based on Renaissance notions of classical design, rather than on the original Greek or Roman. The new dome was essentially completed by 1862.

A Young Washingtonian's Journal 1850-1852, Francis O. French

Francis O. French grew up on Capitol Hill at a time when extensive construction projects were in the works, very much transforming the area within view of his house. As an extremely bright young fellow of thirteen, his observations on the progress and architecture are noteworthy and charming. He was perhaps more interested in the buildings than most boys his age because his father, Benjamin Brown French, was a Commissioner of Public Buildings. In 1852, Francis left Washington to attend Phillips Exeter Academy in New Hampshire. Following are some of his observations from late 1851 to 1852, with his spelling intact.

Source: Francis O. French, *Growing Up on Capitol Hill*. John J. McDonough, ed., Library of Congress, Washington, D.C., 1997. pp. 28, 38-9, 48-9.

Friday, July 4. Today was laid with all cerimonies the corner stone of the new capatol as it is generally called but in truth the North East Corner of the south wing. The general plan of the capitol will be thus [see illustration by Francis below.] The present chamber for the house of Reps. will be changed to a library and the sesions of that body will be held in the South Wing. So the Senate will be in the North Wing[,] thier [former] room to be used by the supreme court. The corner stone was laid by the president of the United States[,] Mr. Fillmore[,] and Mr. Sec. Webster delivered an oration with his usual ability. Father as grand Master of the District of Columbia presided over the Masonic cerimonies as he had prieviou[s]ly done both at the laying of the Corner Stones of the Smithsonian in May 1847 and at the National Monument on the 4th of July 1848—three years previously.

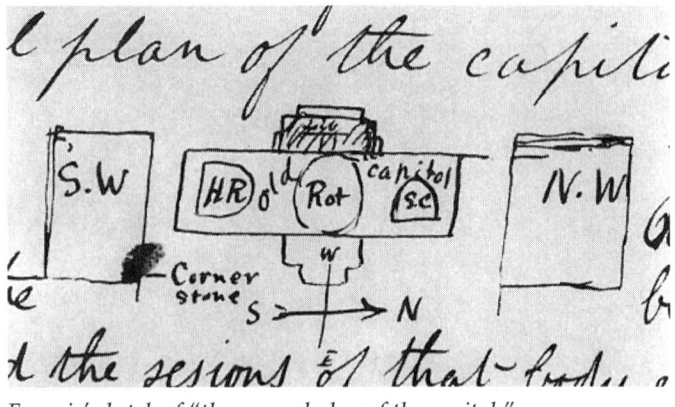

Francis' sketch of "the general plan of the capitol."

Fifty years ago the corner stone of old Capitol was laid by Geo. Washington as a mason[,] and the identical apron and gavel were used by Father on this second occasion. The plan of the capitol was supposed to be large enough for years to come but in less than two generations the increase of our country has been so great that the present building is not large enough to accomadate the officers of the government. Surely if we "judge the future by the past[,]" for all the petty broils and treason like sentiments expressed[,] the prospect for the future is a glorius one. Although I do not think like some patriotic orator of New York who recently said that he believed before twelve months it would be all United States from The Artic Ocean to Patigonia. But enough for this subject.

....

Wednesday, December 31. Today I went to the Smithsonian Institution where for some hours I read[,] having an excelent time [,]for a good book is truely a companion and I know of nothing which is more entertaining. I hope to repeat this visit freqently.

The two wings of the building are now finished. The east wing contains the lecture room and a labratory of instruments. The west wing the library (may it never share the fate of that of Congress) [which had a fire] and a sort of reading room. The inside is finished with arches of wood covered to represent stone. In the main building the wood arches are put up but not covered. They are all now (scince the fire on the 24th) to be taken down and suplanted by iron ones. Another year now has come to a close and it is two years (though my journal is so thin) scince I commenced this history of my life. Already though these two short years have sped so quick I have in them a seventh of my life although to me it seems almost impossible.

At the end of the year, Francis sums up some of the events of 1851, which will be of interest to the reader who likes to put things in their proper time frame.

But a few short hours are left before the bells will chime in eighteen hundred and fifty two leaving fifty-one's records historical. I will now record a few of the most important events as I have just within a few months commenced my monthly record.

Feb. 15. Shadrach an alleged slave is arrested in Boston.

....

A. 25. The president issues the Cuba proclamation.

May 1. Queen Victoria inaugerates the exhibition of the industry of all nations commonly known as the Worlds Fair.

M. 3d. Great Fire in San Francisco, Cal. 2,500 builds burn.

June 22d. Another great fire (6th) at San Francisco destroys 500 houses burned value $3,000,000.

July 10. M. Daguerre the discoverer of the operation which bears his name dies aged sixty one.

....

Aug. 22. The American yacht America, at Cowes[,] wins the "cup of all nations."

Oct. 11. The world's fair closes.

....

Dec. 2. ...
The Submarine Telegraph has been completed and messages are sent between London & Paris. The event was celebrated by the firing of canon at Dover and Calias; being fired from the opposite side....

Monday, February 16. The Dr. and I today went to the Washington National Monument. We saw all the blocks sent by different states, towns, and assosiations; Massachusetts, Pennsylvania, and several other states have beautiful blocks. New Bedford sent a block with a whale sculptured on it, very appropriate we thought. The Dr. went up on top but I (as a dutiful son) did not go up. We next went to the office and saw the California block of gold bearing quartz and the one from Minnesota of the red pipe stone, famed for the Indian pipes. The building is now one hundred and four feet high."

The construction of the Washington Monument

The construction of the Washington Monument, which was discussed for many years, was finally begun in 1848. Benjamin Brown French, as Grand Master, District of Columbia Masons, laid the cornerstone on July 4 of that year, using the trowel that George Washington had used in laying the cornerstone of the U.S. Capitol. Work was halted in 1855 because of political wrangling and a lack of funds. The site remained an eyesore until 1876 when Congress decreed that construction would be renewed at public expense. The monument was completed in 1884.

Many Voices and Many Visions

Since America had so little past to draw on, it seemed natural to reach back into the ancient and grand history of other cultures—and to make those images our own. The nineteenth century saw enthusiastic revivals of Greek, Egyptian, and Roman images, as well as Gothic and other European architectural styles. Just past mid-century, American architect Alexander Jackson Davis offered his clients this list to select from: "American Log Cabin, Farm Villa, English Cottage, Collegiate Gothic, Manor House, French Suburban, Switz Chalet, Switz Mansion, Lombard Italian, Tuscan from Pliny's Villa at Ostia, Ancient Etruscan, Suburban Greek, Oriental, Moorish..." and others.

(Cited in Alan Gowans, *Images of American Living: Four Centuries of Architecture and Furniture as Cultural Expression*, New York, J.B. Lippencott, 1964, p. 303.)

Thomas Cole, "The Architect's Dream," 1840, Toledo Museum of Art (Purchased with funds from Florence Scott Libbey Bequest in Memory of her Father, Maurice A. Scott, 1949). In this 7 foot-wide painting, an architect reclines with closed eyes before a panoramic view of buildings in Egyptian, Roman, Greek, and Gothic styles. The ancient Mediterranean styles are seen in glowing light and the Gothic in shadow (possibly to suggest the Dark Ages).

Greek or Roman?

Not all of the architects who designed buildings with classical columns agreed on the best source for their images. Greek styles were older and simpler, and often considered more dignified. Roman buildings offered additional styles of columns as well as arches and domes—and they were more monumental.

Source: Robert Mills, "The Architectural Works of Robert Mills," an outline for an intended paper or book. Cited in Don Gifford, ed., *The Literature of Architecture: The Evolution of Architectural Theory and Practice in Nineteenth-Century America*, New York: E.P. Dutton, 1966, p. 88.

Mr. Jefferson was an amateur and a great admirer of architecture. He was therefore much gratified to find an American turning his attention to its study, and he gave him every encouragement in the pursuit of his profession. Through his recommendation and advice, the author entered into the office of that celebrated architect and engineer Benjamin H. Latrobe, whom Mr. Jefferson had lately appointed Surveyor of the Public Buildings. With this gentleman, the author pursued and completed his studies and practiced in both branches of his profession, as Mr. Latrobe was, at this time, acting engineer of the Chesapeake and Delaware Canal.

The talents of this gentleman were of the first order; his style was purely Greek, and for the first time in this country was it introduced by him in the Bank of Pennsylvania—a building much admired for its chasteness of design and execution.

It was fortunate that this style was so early introduced into our country, both on the ground of economy and of correct taste, as it exactly suited the character of our political institutions and pecuniary means. Mr. Jefferson was a Roman in his views of architecture, as evidenced in Monticello House, his late residence, which was designed by him, and for the execution of which he furnished with his own hands all the detail drawings.

The example and influence of Mr. Jefferson at first oper-
ated in favor of the introduction of the Roman style into the
country, and it required all the talents and good taste of such
a man as Mr. Latrobe to correct it by introducing a better. The
natural good taste and the unprejudiced eye of our citizens
required only a few examples of the Greek style to convince
them of its superiority over the Roman for public structures,
and its simplicity recommended its introduction into their
private dwellings.

What About Homes?

*The styles in use for public buildings were all applied to private homes at
one time or another. Andrew Jackson Downing was a horticulturist and
landscape architect who designed the landscaping for the nation's Capitol,
the White House, and the Smithsonian Institution. Feeling that people could
not live comfortably in the grand structures suitable for public buildings,
Downing wrote several very influential books on the design of homes.*

Source: Andrew Jackson Downing, *The Architecture of Country Houses*, New York, 1850.
Cited in Don Gifford, *op. cit.*, pp. 218-220.

Domestic architecture is perfect only when it is composed
so as to express the utmost beauty and truth in the life of the
individual....

Architectural style is only exhibited in its severity and per-
fection in public buildings of the first class, whose dignity,
grandeur, and importance demand and permit it; such as the
church, the capitol, public institutions, etc. In them we see, for
example, the Gothic or Greek styles, in their greatest complete-
ness and fullest development. Domestic architecture, on the
contrary, should be less severe, less rigidly scientific, and it
should exhibit more of the freedom and play of feeling of
everyday life. A man may, in public halls, recite a poem in
blank verse, or deliver a studied oration with the utmost pro-

priety; but he would be justly the object of ridicule if at the fireside he talked about the weather, his family, or his friend in the same strain. What familiar conversation, however tasteful and well bred, is to public declamation, domestic is to civil or ecclesiastical architecture; and we have no more patience with those architects who give us copies of the temple of Theseus, with its high, severe colonnades, for dwellings, than with a friend who should describe his wife and children to us in the lofty rhythm of Ossian.

Downing discussed the ideal practical arrangement of spaces in houses, but two women authors got more specific. Harriet Beecher Stowe is known today for her book, Uncle Tom's Cabin. *Later, she and her sister Catharine wrote* The American Woman's Home, *to define exactly what a house should be on the inside. They detailed everything from general layout to the arrangements of drawers and cupboards to heat and ventilation. They even discussed arrangements for the care of children, the aged, servants, and the sick. Both women clearly believed that a woman's interests lay in the home—but that women's duties should be given as much consideration as those of men. The forward to their book is excepted below. In their book, they went on to explain how their perspective affected the design of a house.*

Source: C. Beecher and H.B. Stowe, *The American Woman's Home*, New York: 1869. Cited in Leland M. Roth, *America Builds: Source Documents in American Architecture and Planning*, New York: Harper and Row, 1983, pp. 57-58.

The authors of this volume, while they sympathize with every honest effort to relieve the disabilities and sufferings of their sex, are confident that the chief cause of these evils is the fact that the honor and duties of the family state are not duly appreciated, that women are not trained for these duties as men are trained for their trades and professions, and that, as the consequence, family labor is poorly done, poorly paid, and regarded as menial and disgraceful.

To be the nurse of young children, a cook, or a housemaid, is regarded as the lowest and last resort of poverty, and one which no woman of culture and position can assume without loss of caste and respectability.

It is the aim of this volume to elevate both the honor and the remuneration of all the employments that sustain the many difficult and sacred duties of the family state, and thus to render each department of woman's true profession as much desired and respected as are the most honored professions of men.

When the other sex are to be instructed in law, medicine, or divinity, they are favored with numerous institutions richly endowed, with teachers of the highest talents and acquirements, with extensive libraries, and abundant and costly apparatus. With such advantages they devote nearly ten of the best years of life to preparing themselves for their profession; and to secure the public from unqualified members of these professions, none can enter them until examined by a competent body, who certify to their due preparation for their duties.

Woman's profession embraces the care and nursing of the body in the critical periods of infancy and sickness, the training of the human mind in the most impressible period of childhood, the instruction and control of servants, and most of the government and economies of the family state. These duties of woman are as sacred and important as any ordained to man; and yet no such advantages for preparation have been accorded to her, nor is there any qualified body to certify the public that a woman is duly prepared to give proper instruction in her profession.

Old or New?

As discussions raged over the uses of Greek, Roman, Gothic or other ancient images, it did occur to some architects that a brand new style could be developed in the United States. Others disagreed.

Some of the very designers working in classical styles considered the possibility of other options.

Source: Robert Mills, "The Progress of Architecture in Virginia," an unfinished essay the original of which is in the possession of the Dimitry family. Cited in Don Gifford, *op. cit.*, p. 84.

I say to our artists: Study your country's tastes and requirements, and make classic ground here for your art. Go not to the Old World for your examples. We have entered a new era in the history of the world; it is our destiny to lead, not to be led. Our vast country is before us and our motto Excelsior. The importance of the subject must plead for this digression.

Sculptor Horatio Greenough's statue of George Washington (made for the Capitol building and now in the Smithsonian), showed the first president bare to the waist in the Roman costume. Although he later entertained ideas of a more uniquely American style, he seemed pessimistic about the possibilities of actual innovation.

Source: Horatio Greenough, *The Travels, Observations, and Experience of a Yankee Stonecutter*, New York: 1852. Cited in Don Gifford, *op. cit.*, p 141.

We have heard the learned in matters relating to art express the opinion that these United States are destined to form a new style of architecture. Remembering that a vast population, rich in material and guided by the experience, the precepts, and the models of the Old World, was about to erect durable structures for every function of civilized life, we also cherished the hope that such a combination would speedily be formed.

We forgot that though the country was young, yet the people were old, that as Americans we have no childhood, no half-fabulous, legendary wealth, no misty, cloud-enveloped background. We forgot that we had not unity of religious belief, nor unity of origin; that our territory, extending from the white bear to the alligator, made our occupations dissimilar, our character and tastes various. We forgot that the Republic had leaped full-grown and armed to the teeth from the brain of her parent, and that a hammer had been the instrument of delivery. We forgot that reason had been the dry nurse of the giant offspring, and had fed her from the beginning with the stout bread and meat of fact....

Reason can dissect, but cannot originate; she can adopt, but cannot create; she can modify, but cannot find....She can initiate the flush of the young cheek, but where is the flash of the young eye? She buys the teeth-alas! she cannot buy the breath of childhood.

Calvert Vaux, architect, engineer, and landscape architect, was the partner and successor of A.J. Downing. Like Greenough, he didn't see any likelihood of new developments.

Source: Calvert Vaux, *Villas and Cottages*, New York, 1857. Cited in Don Gifford, *op. cit.*, p. 241.

When the talent and energy that are fostered by American institutions are distributed with tolerable fairness, we shall, among many other things, be justified in expecting to find in every architectural effort, not something so new that it is unintelligible, but some distinctive characteristics that show it to be a genuine American invention. These, however, can hardly be expected to depend much on the employment of really new forms....

All previous experience in architecture is the inherited property of America, and should be taken every advantage of. Each beautiful thought, form, and mode that is not unsuited to the climate and the people ought to be studied, and tested, its principles elucidated, and itself improved on; but the past should always be looked on as a servant, not as a master.

The lecturer, essayist, and poet, Ralph Waldo Emerson noted that originality requires passion.

Source: Ralph Waldo Emerson, "Thoughts on Art," *The Dial*, Vol. I., No. III, pp. 367-368, Boston, January 1841. Cited in Don Gifford, *op. cit,.* p. 109.

The Gothic cathedrals were built when the builder and the priest and the people were overpowered by their faith. Love and fear laid every stone. The Madonnas of Raphael and Titian were made to be worshipped. Tragedy was instituted for the like purpose, and the miracles of music—all sprang out of some genuine enthusiasm, and never out of dilettantism and holidays. But now they languish, because their purpose is merely exhibition. Who cares, who knows what works of art our government has ordered to be made for the Capitol? They are a mere flourish to please the eye of persons who have associations with books and galleries....

In this country, at this time, other interests than religion and patriotism are predominant, and the arts, the daughters of enthusiasm, do not flourish. The genuine offspring of our ruling passions we behold. Popular institutions, the school, the reading room, the post office, the exchange, the insurance company, and an immense harvest of economical inventions are the fruit of the equality and the boundless liberty of lucrative callings. These are superficial wants; and their fruits are these superficial institutions. But as far as they accelerate the end of political freedom and national education, they are preparing the soil of man for fairer flowers and fruits in another age. For beauty, truth, and goodness are not obsolete; they spring eternal in the breast of man; they are as indigenous in Massachusetts as in Tuscany or the Isles of Greece.

Change in Chicago

The passion that could produce innovation wasn't lacking in America. Here and there in larger cities, some architects were developing new ideas as they searched for ways to express the energy, achievements, and ambitions of emerging business and industry. In Chicago, a disaster gave them room to work.

Source: *Picturesque Chicago and Guide to the World's Fair*, Baltimore: R.H. Woodward, 1892, pp. 26-27. The quoted passage is identified as being from Mr. Kirkland's "Story of Chicago."

Chicago had then a population of about 334,000....

"The fire Of 1871, broke out on Sunday night, October 8th. There had been on the previous evening an extensive conflagration in the west division, involving a heavy loss of property in the lumber district. The firemen had worked upon the blaze for many hours, finally succeeding in subduing it. The department, however, was pretty well exhausted when an alarm was sounded at nine o'clock on the following Sunday evening. The fire was caused by the upsetting of a little lamp, in a stable....Whether the lamp was kicked over by a cow belonging to Mrs. O'Leary is a question that has never been satisfactorily settled...."

The total area burned over was nearly three and a third square miles; number of buildings destroyed, 17,450; persons rendered homeless, 98,500; persons killed, about 200; loss, not including the depreciation of real estate or loss of business, estimated at $190,000,000; recovered by insurance, $44,000,000. One year after the fire many of the best business blocks were rebuilt; five years after the fire the city was handsomer and more prosperous than ever; ten years after the fire nearly all traces of the calamity had disappeared.

Far from being permanently devastated by the fire, Chicago was an energetic town again in 1873, according to novelist Theodore Dreiser.

Source: Theodore Dreiser, *The Titan*, New York:World Publishing, 1925, p. 6.

This singing flame of a city, this all America, this poet in chaps and buckskin, this rude, raw Titan, this Burns of a city! By its shimmering lake it lay, a king of shreds and patches, a maundering yokel with an epic in its mouth, a tramp, a hobo among cities, with the grip of Caesar in its mind, the dramatic force of Euripedes in its soul. A very bard of a city this, singing of high deeds and high hopes, its heavy Brogans buried deep in the mire of circumstance. Take Athens, oh, Greece! Italy, do you keep Rome! This was the Babylon, the Troy, the Nineveh of a younger day. Here came the gaping West and the hopeful East to see. Here hungry men, raw from the shops and fields, idyls and romances in their minds, builded them an empire crying glory in the mud.

The city embarked on a rebuilding program, using stone to replace wooden buildings and creating one of the first modern fire departments in America. The Chicago architects began to base their images on new building techniques. By mid-century, American architect James Bogardus had erected cast iron and iron and glass buildings in New York. In 1851, the Crystal Palace was built of iron and glass for the Great Exposition in London. Construction was begun on the Brooklyn Bridge in 1869 (it went on until 1883).

Those innovations made taller buildings possible; another made them practical. Elisha Graves Otis designed a safety device for elevators and installed the first passenger elevator in a New York City store in 1857. By 1889, electric motors made the originally steam-powered elevators even more useful.

Burnam and Root's 1891 Monadnock Building reached skyward without the benefit of decoration of any kind—an entirely new look in American architecture. Courtesy of Chicago Architectural Photographing Company.

Young and talented architects such Louis Henry Sullivan and John Well-born Root were drawn to Chicago, where they experimented with designs for commercial buildings of enormous size. By the early 1890's, the city was a showcase for a new American style—the skyscraper.

Source: C.H. Blackall, "Notes of Travel. Chicago. III," *American Architect* 23, February 25, 1888, p. 89. Cited in David F. Burg, *Chicago's White City of 1893*, Lexington, Kentucky: University of Kentucky Press, 1976, p. 53.

It goes without saying that the buildings are grand and imposing. No structure can be erected covering the area that these do, and carried up into the air ten or twelve stories, without being majestic and awe-inspiring....Such structures seemed more than human. One such building is imposing, but a whole street of such huge structures seems like the work of giants.

The Return of Rome -
The Columbian Exposition

Chicago is Chosen and Work Begins

In spite of the new structures in Chicago, Rome returned in full force for the Columbian Exposition—a world's fair held in 1893 to celebrate the 400th anniversary of Columbus' arrival in the New World.

Source: Benjamin C. Truman, *History of The World's Fair: Being A Complete and Authentic Description of the Columbian Exposition from Its Inception*, Philadelphia: H.W. Kelley, 1893. Reprinted, Daniel J. Boorstin, ed., New York: Arno Press, 1976, pp. 23-24.

As soon as it became evident that the World's Fair would be a coveted honor and that rivalry among the leading cities of America for the distinction of holding it would be keen, Chicago prepared to get it. The City Council passed a resolution July 22, 1889, instructing the mayor to appoint a committee of one hundred to induce Congress to locate the Fair in Chicago....

How bitterly the battle was waged between east and west all the world knows. Nothing that could influence the decision of Congress was left undone. Nothing that the press could contribute toward the settlement of the problem was left unwritten. It was, therefore, a signal endorsement of Chicago's persistency and pluck, when in the face of the opposition of the representatives of the Eastern interests Congress voted, February 24, 1890, to have the Exposition in Chicago.

Buildings were to be built—but first architects had to be chosen and land prepared.

Source: Benjamin C. Truman, *op cit.*, pp. 641-66.

The next step was the selection of architects to design the buildings, and the committee authorized Mr. Burnham to select five architects outside of the city of Chicago to design the five principal buildings around the court. Later Mr. Burnham was authorized to appoint five architects from Chicago to design the remaining buildings which had been determined on. The committee determined, however, to select an architect for the Woman's Building by competition, to be confined strictly to women. By March 1, 1891, the chief of construction having apportioned the work among the architects, was enabled to form an estimate of the work to be done by his department. Roughly speaking, it consisted of reclaiming nearly seven hundred acres of ground, only a small portion of which was improved, the remainder being in a state of nature, and covered with water and wild-oak ridges, and in twenty months converting it from a sedgy waste by the borders of an inland sea, into a site suitable in substance and decoration for an exposition of the industries and the entertainment by the republic of representatives of all the nations of the world. On its stately terraces a dozen palaces were to be built—all of great extent and highest architectural importance—these to be supplemented by hundreds of other structures, some of which were to be almost the size of the Exposition buildings themselves; great canals, basins, lagoons, and islands were to be formed, extensive docks, bridges, and towers to be constructed. The standard of the entire work was to be kept up to a degree of excellence which should place it upon a level with the monuments of other ages....

That Question of Image

What would the buildings look like? How would designs be selected for such a grand undertaking? Writer Frank D. Millet describes the process.

Source: Frank D. Millet, "The Decoration of the Exposition," in *Some Artists at the Fair*, New York: Charles Scribner's Sons, 1893, p. 6.

Mr. D. H. Burnham, the Director of Works of the World's Columbian Exposition, took the first important step toward the renaissance of the true spirit of architecture in this country by ignoring all precedents of competition, and selecting as associates certain architects and firms whose records established their position as true leaders of the profession. These architects, after studious contemplation of the Situation, decided on the adoption of a general classical style for the buildings, subject, of course, to such modifications as were found necessary by the requirements of each individual case.

So the buildings of the World's Columbian Exposition were to reflect the Roman and Greek image favored for the past hundred years. Some of the same architects who experimented with bold and innovative skyscraper design right there in Chicago also participated in this celebration of the classical image.

Henry Van Brunt was instrumental in establishing architecture as a profession in America. An architect, a teacher, and a writer, he was sympathetic with the decision that Burnham and the committee made.

Source: Henry Van Brunt, "World's Columbian Exposition," *Architecture and Society: Selected Essays of Henry Van Brunt*, William A. Coles, ed., Cambridge: Harvard University Press, 1969, p. 233.

In view of the fact that these buildings had a mutual dependence much more marked than any others on the grounds, and that the formal or architectural character of the court absolutely required a perfect harmony of feeling among the five structures which inclose it, it became immediately evident to these gentlemen that they must adopt, not only a uniform and ceremonious style,—a style evolved from, and expressive of, the highest civilizations in history,—in which each one could express himself with fluency, but also a common module of dimension....The style should be distinctly secular and pompous, restrained from license by historical authority, and organized by academical discipline. It was not difficult, therefore, to agree upon the use of Roman classic forms, correctly and loyally interpreted, but permitting variations suggested not only by the Italians, but by the other masters of the Renaissance. It was considered that a series of pure classic models, in each case contrasting in character according to the personal equation of the architect, and according to the practical conditions to be accommodated in each, but uniform in respect to scale and language of form, all set forth with the utmost amount of luxury and opulence of decoration permitted by the best usage, and on a theater of almost unprecedented magnitude, would present to the profession here an object-lesson so impressive of the practical value of architectural scholarship and of strict subordination to the formulas of the schools, that it would serve as a timely corrective to the national tendency to experiments in design. It is not desired or expected that this display, however successful it may prove to be in execution, should make a new revival or a new school in the architecture of our country, or interfere with any healthy advance on classic or romantic lines which may be evolving here....

Although Van Brunt saw the fair buildings as the natural expression of America's lofty aspirations, he assumed that they would not have a permanent effect on the course of architecture in America. He noted that "real" architecture could be found quite nearby.

Source: Henry Van Brunt, *op. cit.*, p 232.

Probably the largest, the most deliberate, and the most conspicuous expression of the present condition of architecture in this country will be looked for by foreign critics on the grounds of the World's Columbian Exposition; but they will find it rather in the latest commercial, educational, and domestic structures in and near our larger cities. By these our architecture should be judged. It is true that the industrial palaces of our exposition will be larger in area than any which have preceded them, and will surpass in this respect even the imperial villas and baths of the ancient Romans. But they will be an unsubstantial pageant of which the concrete elements will be a series of vast covered inclosures, adjusted on architectural plans to the most lucid classification and the most effective arrangement of the materials of the Exposition, and faced with a decorative mask of plaster composition on frames of timber and iron, as the Romans of the Empire clothed their rough structures of cement and brick with magnificent architectural veneers of marbles, bronze, and sculpture. Mr. Burnham, the Chief of Construction, rubs his wonderful lamp of Aladdin in his office at Chicago, and the sudden result is an exhalation, a vast phantasm of architecture, glittering with domes, towers, and banners…which presently will fade and leave no trace behind.

Short-term Pomp

Frank Millet also mentioned one drawback—his "regret and disappointment that they are not to remain as monuments to the good taste, knowledge and skill of the men who built them, and as a permanent memorial of the event which the Exposition is intended to celebrate."
Source: Millet, *op. cit.*, p. 1-20.

Van Brunt also reminded readers of the temporary nature of the White City.

Source: Henry Van Brunt, *op. cit.*, p 234.

It must be borne in mind, however, that all this is not architecture in its highest sense, but rather a scenic display of architecture, composed (to use a theatrical term) of "practicable" models, executed on a colossal stage, and with a degree of apparent pomp and splendor which, if set forth in marbles and bronze, might recall the era of Augustus or Nero.

Late 19th century American ambitions were expressed in monumental classical images for the Columbian Exposition.

Most of the structures in the Columbian Exposition were not permanent. They were mostly made of "staff"—a kind of plaster of Paris mixed with gypsum and fibers. Some of the buildings showed signs of decay even before the fair ended.

Source: F.D. Millet, "The Designers of the Fair," *Harper's New Monthly Magazine* 85, November 1892, p. 143.

"[Staff] permitted them, in fact to indulge in an architectural spree...of a magnitude never before attempted; it made it possible to make a colossal sketch of a group of buildings which no autocrat and no government could ever have carried out in permanent form; it left them free, finally, to reproduce with fidelity and accuracy the best details of ancient architecture, to erect temples, colonnades, towers, and domes of surpassing beauty and of noble proportions..."

The Women's Building was one of the more reserved structures at the Exposition. There were only three known female architects in the United States at the time, and the design competition was won by Sophia G. Hayden. Many critics found the building unimpressive, but others admired its more human scale.

Wonder and Wonder

Like Van Brunt, Henry Adams thought that the fair was likely to represent a new direction for America.

Source: Henry Adams, *op. cit.*, pp. 324-325.

He set off to Chicago to study the Exposition again, and stayed there a fortnight absorbed in it. He found matter of study to fill a hundred years, and his education spread over chaos, Indeed it seemed to him as though, this year, education went mad....The Exposition itself defied philosophy. One might find fault till the last gate closed, one could still explain nothing that needed explanation. As a scenic display, Paris had never approached it, but the inconceivable scenic display consisted in its being there at all—more surprising, as it was, than anything else on the continent, Niagara Falls, the Yellowstone Geysers and the whole railway system thrown in, since these were all natural products in their place; while, since Noah's Ark, no such Babel of loose and ill-joined, such vague and ill-defined and unrelated thoughts and half-thoughts and experimental outcries as the Exposition, had ever ruffled the surface of the lakes.

The first astonishment became greater every day....Was the American made to seem at home in it? Honestly, he had the air of enjoying it as though it were all his own; he felt it was good; he was proud of it; for the most part, he acted as though he had passed his life in landscape gardening and architectural decoration. If he had not done it himself, he had known how to get it done to suit him, as he knew how to get his wives and daughters dressed at Worth's or Paquin's. Perhaps he could not do it again; the next time he would want to do it himself and would show his own faults; but for the moment he seemed to have leaped directly from Corinth and Syracuse and Venice, over the heads of London and New York, to impose classical standards on plastic Chicago....

One sat down to ponder on the steps beneath Richard Hunt's dome almost as deeply as on the steps of Ara Coeli, and much to the same purpose. Here was a breach of continuity, a rupture in historical sequence! Was it real, or only apparent? One's personal universe hung on the answer, for, if the rupture was real and the new American world could take this sharp and conscious twist towards ideals, one's personal friends would come in, at last, as winners in the great American chariot-race for fame. If the people of the Northwest actually knew what was good when they saw it, they would some day talk about Hunt and Richardson, La Farge and St Gaudens, Burnham and McKim, and Stanford White when their politicians and millionaires were otherwise forgotten.

The artists and architects who had done the work offered little encouragement to hope it; they talked freely enough, but not in terms that one cared to quote; and to them the Northwest refused to look artistic. They talked as though they worked only for themselves; as though art, to the Western people, was a stage decoration; a diamond shirt-stud; a paper collar; but possibly the architects of Paestum and Girgenti had talked in the same way, and the Greek had said the same thing of Semitic Carthage two thousand years ago....

American novelist William Dean Howells wrote a series of essays in the form of commentaries of a traveler from a fictional country called Altruria. Of course the Altrurian traveler visited the Columbian Exposition, discussed it with a person he met there, and wrote to a friend about the experience.

Source: William Dean Howells, *Letters of An Altrurian Traveller (1893-94)*, a facsimile reproduction with an introduction by Clara M. Kirk and Rudolf Kirk, Gainesville, Florida: Scholars' Facsimiles & Reprints, 1961, p. 32.

Chicago, Sept. 28, 1893

I heartily agreed with him in condemning the most that had yet been done in architecture in America, but I tried to make him observe that the simplicity of Greek architecture came out of the simplicity of Greek life, and the preference given in the Greek state to the intellectual over the industrial, to art over business. I pointed out that until there was some enlightened municipal or national control of the matter, no excellence of example could avail, but that the classicism of the Fair City would become, among a wilful and undisciplined people, a fad with the rich and a folly with the poor, and not a real taste with either class....I ventured so far as to say that the whole competitive world, with the exception of a few artists, had indeed lost the sense of beauty, and I even added that the Americans as a people seemed never to have had it at all.

He was not offended, as I had feared he might be, but asked me with perfect good nature what I meant.

"Why, I mean that the Americans came into the world too late to have inherited the influence from the antique world which was lost even in Europe, when in medieval times the picturesque barbarously substituted itself for the beautiful and a feeling for the quaint grew up in place of love for the perfect."

Frank Lloyd Wright

Frank Lloyd Wright was working in the office of Louis Sullivan at the time of the Columbian Exposition. Wright was later to become globally famous for his innovations in architecture as well as for his essays and speeches on the topic. Wright saw the fair as a disaster for the development of an American image in architecture. Many other architects and critics agreed.

Source: Frank Lloyd Wright, *An Organic Architecture: The Architecture of Democracy, The Sir George Watson Lectures of the Sulgrave Manor Board for 1939,* Cambridge: The M.I.T. Press, 1970.

We were doing fairly well in the States going on toward expression of ourselves as a people with an architecture of our own, when as luck would have it we got our first World's Fair, the World's Fair of 1893. And there, for the first time the United States of America saw architecture as a great orchestration, and loved it, without giving much consideration to its nature, not knowing that it all came to them on tracing paper from dry books, or that as "traditional" it all lay oblique against the grain of our own integral indigenous effort. We had many too-well-educated architects at that time—you know their names, you who are familiar with architecture—and it became quite simple on their part, scholars—all—thus finding architecture ready-made, to sell it on a large scale, conveniently enough, to the American people. Architecture forthwith became a great business in the old forms of grandomania as architects themselves—scholars all—became active brokers....

Therefore, most architecture in our Usonia,[3] after this 1893 World's Fair disaster, was a kind of mongering of that sort. For myself I could never see that such ready-made architecture obtained any great results or had anything to do with our life as our life was lived. I felt sure, even then, that architecture which was really architecture proceeded from the ground and that somehow the terrain, the native industrial conditions, the nature of materials and the purpose of the building, must inevitably determine the form and character of any good building. All this crowding in on the scene, therefore, was a great distress to me. Louis Sullivan, my old master, with whom I had been growing up, had already demonstrated his thought as independent and worthy of the attention of his people but this world's-fair wave of Pseudo "Classic" now an 'ism, swept over and swept us all under. It was years and years before we began to emerge from the undertow of that tremendous back-wash....

I declare, the time is here for architecture to recognise its own nature, to realise the fact that it is out of life itself for life as it is now lived, a humane and therefore an intensely human thing; it must again become the most human of all the expressions of human nature. Architecture is a necessary interpretation of such human life as we now know if we ourselves are to live with individuality and beauty.

The "Classic" of course made no such statement; the "Classic" ideal can allow nothing of the kind to transpire. The "Classic" was more a mask for life to wear than an expression of life itself. Then how much more so was Pseudo-Classic? So modern architecture rejects the major-axis and the minor-axis of classic architecture. It rejects all grandomania, every building that would stand in military fashion heels together, eyes front, something on the right hand

---

[3] Wright used this term for North America.

and something on the left hand. Architecture already favours the reflex, the natural easy attitude, the occult symmetry of grace and rhythm affirming the ease, grace, and naturalness of natural life. Modern architecture—let us now say *organic* architecture—is a natural architecture-the architecture of nature, for Nature.

Frank Lloyd Wright's "Falling Water" house is part of its natural surroundings.

Epilogue

For about forty years after the Columbian Exposition, a public building in America had to be white and it had to have columns. Businesses that wanted to project a serious image— such as banks— followed the same style. But eventually the innovations of architects in Chicago and other cities captured the attention of the world. As the twentieth century progressed, stark and simple modern images came into worldwide vogue. Those huge glass boxes were followed by a variety of more unique forms, as well as by new uses of images from the past. These days, American architects are called upon to create new styles.

Now the most familiar American image is probably that of New York City skyscrapers—paying homage to the power of business and finance rather than to ancient temples.

Lewis Hine photographed the construction of the Empire State Building in 1930, with New York City skyscrapers in the background.

Suggested Further Reading

Applebaum, Stanley. *The Chicago World's Fair of 1893: A Photographic Record*. New York: Dover, 1980.

Burg, David F. *Chicago's White City of 1893*. Lexington, Kentucky: University of Kentucky Press, 1976.

Bushong, William B., et. al. *Uncle Sam's Architects: Builders of the Capitol*. Washington, D.C.: United States Capitol Historical Society, 1994.

Butler, Jeanne F. "Competition 1792: Designing a Nation's Capitol," *Capitol Studies*, Vol. 4, Number 1, 1976.

French, Francis O., John J. McDonough, ed. *Growing Up on Capitol Hill, A Young Washingtonian's Journal, 1850-1852*. Washington, D.C.: Library of Congress, 1997.

Gifford, Don, ed. *The Literature of Architecture: The Evolution of Architectural Theory and Practice in Nineteenth-Century America*. New York: E.P. Dutton, 1966.

Gowans, Alan. *Images of American Living: Four Centuries of Architecture and Furniture as Cultural Expression*. New York: J.B. Lippincott, 1964.

Jefferson, Thomas. *Writings*. Merrill D. Peterson, ed. New York: Library Classics of the United States, 1984.

Kennedy Roger G. *Hidden Cities: The Discovery and Loss of Ancient North American Civilization*. New York: The Free Press (Macmillan, Inc.), 1994.

Kimball, Fiske. *The Capitol of Virginia: A Landmark of American Architecture*. John Kukla, ed. Richmond: Virginia State Library and Archives, 1989.

Lieberthal, Mary Loucheim. *Designing a Nation's Capitol: Controversy and Compromise*. New Orleans Museum of Art. 1976.

Roth, Leland M. *America Builds: Source Documents in American Architecture and Planning*. New York: Harper and Row, 1983.

About the Editor

Pat Perrin is a freelance writer who lives in Chapel Hill, North Carolina. With her husband, Wim Coleman, she has collaborated on two novels and a nonfiction book for major trade publishers, as well as numerous works for educational publishers. *Terminal Games*, their suspense thriller about computer networking, was published by Bantam Books in 1994. Foreign language editions have appeared in Japan, Germany, Italy, and Brazil.

Both Pat and Wim have edited and introduced several other titles for Discovery Enterprises, Ltd.'s *Perspectives on History Series*, including *The Shakers; The American Quakers; The Age of Broadcasting: Radio; The Age of Broadcasting: Television;* and *The Declaration of Independence.*